D1327856

# Playing for Celtic

# PLAYING FOR CELTIC

Edited by RODGER BAILLIE

STANLEY PAUL, LONDON

STANLEY PAUL & CO LTD
*3 Fitzroy Square, London W1*

AN IMPRINT OF THE HUTCHINSON GROUP

London Melbourne Sydney Auckland
Wellington Johannesburg Cape Town
and agencies throughout the world

*First Published 1973*

*This book has been set in Baskerville, printed in Great Britain
by offset litho by Flarepath Printers Ltd., St. Albans, Herts.
and bound by William Brendon of Tiptree, Essex*

ISBN 0 09 117170 9

# Contents

# What a Record!

THERE have never been more impressive statistics in the history of Scottish football . . . for it has never happened before!

A look at the league table of Celtic's eight successive championship victories shows a combined total of:

Played 272 games. Won 212, lost 22, drawn 38. Goals for 786, against 231 and total points 462.

That eighth championship win was the supreme highlight in a season which provided more than its usual mixture of success and failure.

The success of it was all the sweeter for the championship victory was achieved in spite of a powerful and sustained challenge from Celtic's perpetual rivals, Rangers.

It meant re-writing yet again of another chapter in the soccer history books. For no sooner had the achievement in winning a seventh championship been hailed as creating a new record than it was to be changed again.

After the seventh win the Scottish Football league honoured the club at a special dinner, attended by representatives of every League Club in Scotland, for making that unique bit of history.

Then the club made it even more impressive with the eighth win. And the margin of their success with the championship had become so overwhelming that it now stretched back to the middle sixties.

Long enough for a sad decline in the fortune of the team who had won it last before Celtic's domination started. Kilmarnock ended season 1972–73 by being relegated.

The League dinner was one of the highlights in a series of honours paid to the players and officials of Celtic during a busy season.

There was another special testimonial dinner, this time organized by a group of businessmen to the man who was responsible for so much of the success, manager Jock Stein.

The flags of victory . . . as Celtic fans hail their team's championship win after Hibs at Easter Road.

It was made memorable by a witty and warm tribute to him from one of his closest friends in football, Liverpool manager Bill Shankley.

And there was also a generous gesture by the club to the manager's wife, when Celtic chairman Desmond White presented a bracelet to Mrs. Jean Stein.

Another honour was paid to the club by the members of the Scottish Football Writers' Association, who awarded their coveted annual 'Player of the Year' trophy to George Connelly.

It was a recognition of a season's soccer by Connelly which had seen him finally emerge from being one of the club's bright young players to an elegant and outstanding peak.

There were also two major honours to Celtic from Britain's most famous footballing brothers, Bobby and Jackie Charlton.

Both of them retired at the end of the season after long and distinguished careers, and both had impressive testimonial matches arranged for them.

Bobby Charlton was first last autumn when Celtic played to a packed Old Trafford crowd, and drew 0–0 with Manchester

10     . . . The struggle in an 'Old Firm' match . . . shown as Rangers and Celtic players keep their eye firmly on that ball during a league game.

United in a match which always had absorbing interest.

But the manner of Celtic's approach to such a fixture—they went out to play with twin targets of a competitive approach and also a football flourish — impressed Jack Charlton immensely.

He did not wait for formal invitations but scrapped earlier plans he had made for his benefit match to make a quick approach for Celtic at the banquet after brother Bobby's game.

The only date that could be found for it in the tight demanding end of the season schedule was two days after the Scottish and English Cup Finals.

Both teams, Celtic and Leeds United, reached their respective finals, but two sides called Rangers and Sunderland shattered the plans for the two Cups to be paraded at the game.

Yet perhaps because both Celtic and Leeds had been beaten in the finals it was more of a tribute to the teams that they shrugged aside the numbing hangover of defeat to produce a game at Elland Road which was numbered among the highlights of the season for so many people.

The shooting power of Jimmy Johnstone . . . as he slams this shot into goal during a game against Dundee.    11

Celtic won the game 4–3, thanks to a late goal by Jimmy Johnstone, but the score-line seemed almost incidental in such a feast of good football.

The match also raised the perpetual question which arises every time Celtic play in England . . . how would they manage in the Football League.

Jock Stein, realistic as ever, pointed out that it was an idea which he considered would always remain a dream, for football's legislators were unlikely to adopt it.

But he was in no doubt that his team would challenge strongly in such a set-up. He said that entry every season into the European Cup would disappear . . . Celtic could not hope to win a competitive British League eight times on the trot.

But the Celtic boss declared that would be balanced by the adrenalin of playing to full houses every league game of the season.

And he would rather have it that way, with one championship perhaps in six years in a British League than the present Scottish set-up, which he has frequently said must be re-formed.

Any season also has its share of failures, the sweets of victory would not taste so well for any team if they had a total monopoly.

For Celtic the failures curiously came in the competitions which, until their league successes, they had always seemed superior. I mean the short, sharp sprints which with three, four or five games can win a team a Cup.

The lack of success started with a defeat by Hibs in the pre-season Drybrough Cup, a swashbuckling fixture which went to extra time and the Edinburgh side eventually won 5–3.

Then came another defeat by Hibs, this time by 2–1 in the final of the League Cup, which was played in December.

And sandwiched in between these two was a quick boot out the European Cup, in only the second round, by the impressive side, Ujpest Dozsa.

This was the defeat which affected the club most during the middle part of the season. Only once before in seven European campaigns had they failed to reach the elite last eight in the European Cup quarter-finals.

The last Cup loss was in the final competitive fixture of the season, a 3–2 dumping by Rangers in the Scottish Cup Final.

It was also a season marked by dramatic events off the field. There was the illness of manager Jock Stein, when he was taken into a Glasgow hospital with a heart complaint caused by the burden of his heavy schedule. Happily he was soon to completely recover.

12    It's a Fifer v. East Fife. As Celtic's forward Tommy Callaghan, who comes from near Dunfermline, tries to pierce the East Fife defence at Parkhead.

There was the emergence of chairman Desmond White as one of the most impressive legislators in Scottish football.

He showed he was not afraid to stand up and say what he thought of the many issues and the many ills which affect Scottish football as the sport fights to keep the fans from drifting away.

But plain speaking has not been much in fashion in the Scottish Football Association in recent seasons, the men who shelter behind the timid 'no comment' have taken over.

And when he stood for the post of S.F.A. treasurer, the third most important office in their pecking order, he was defeated and retired, hopefully only temporarily from the S.F.A. Council.

Scottish football has few enough voices prepared to stand up and speak out, they cannot afford to silence them.

Another off-the-field event was the sudden shock transfer request by Lou Macari, which saw a fight to sign him by Manchester United, then bottom of the English League, and Liverpool, who were at the top, and won by United's new boss, ex-Scotland Team Manager Tommy Docherty.

14    Nice one, Dixie! And Celtic's centre heads another of the many goals he scored during the season.

But Macari's loss was not felt as keenly as it might have been. For the near £200,000 transfer fee was used to strengthen Celtic's side with the buying of three players.

The one who quickly proved one of the season's most effective buys was goalkeeper Alistair Hunter, signed from Kilmarnock where he had been dropped to the reserves.

He ended the season with a championship medal, and his place back in the Scotland side for the match against England at Wembley where he had a triumphant game.

The other two signings were winger Andy Lynch, who unfortunately was haunted by injury, and an end of season signing, Steve Murray from Aberdeen, whom manager Stein looked to strengthen his mid-field.

They were new faces, but the ambition was still the same as the old . . . to keep their club at the very forefront of Scottish soccer.

# An Eightsome Reel

THE supporters' scarves and banners were waving from every corner of Easter Road. It was a mass of green and white as the fans hailed yet another league championship victory for Celtic.

Seconds before the referee John Gordon had blown his final blast to signal the last league game of the season, and Celtic's emphatic 3–0 victory against Hibs had sealed an eighth championship triumph.

Down on the pitch the Celtic players fell into each others arms, broad smiles split their faces as they set off for the ritual lap of honour which now seems as much part of Scotland's spring soccer scene as any date written in the calendar.

This time they brought a novel touch to the parade. For the players applauded the fans, the men and women on the terraces who had pushed them towards the league title.

Down on the Celtic trainer's bench a little drama had been unfolding as the game rushed to a close. The photographers had crowded round the bench waiting for the end of the match, and Jock Stein rising off it in triumph. But that cunning fox tricked them, by simply getting off his seat and walking up the tunnel at the final whistle as calmly as if he had watched the end of a training session.

As the chants of 'Jock Stein' rolled round the ground he stood later, half-hidden at the entrance to the tunnel, to watch his team take their bow.

They deserved it. Yet another page of league championship history had been re-written again. For a record-breaking seven now read a record-breaking eight.

Maybe it was something to which we were too close. Maybe it will need football's future historians to turn back to it one day and weigh it all up properly.

Yet it would probably be fair to say that in all the cheers that

16

greeted the victory, in all the backslapping that went on among the team there was mixed a measure of relief.

For it had been the championship that had seemed at half-way a foregone conclusion. With the ease of a racing thoroughbred Celtic had zoomed to a five-point lead over the rest of the field.

It seemed only a formality whether the championship ended in February or dragged on to March. Anyone who suggested then that Celtic would have to fight to depend on at least one point from their last game of the season might have been expected to have been led quietly away.

Yet that was the way it worked out. There were two factors, one of them was self-imposed, the other they could not do much about.

The first was their own slip in form in the second half of the season. It hit them just after the New Year and took a couple of months before it travelled through their system.

The other was the amazing run of Rangers. They lost their last league game on 2 December, and dropped only two more points—drawn games against Aberdeen—for the rest of the season.

But at the end Celtic were worthy champions. They had scored the most goals, 93, and conceded the fewest, 28. Those are the kind of statistics from which champions are forged.

And in their last seven games they scored 23 goals, lost only one and took full points to finally edge off Rangers' formidable challenge by only one point.

Despite their slips they finished only three points down on their total for the previous season with 55 points, and they won 26, drew three and lost five games.

The record number of appearances were made by George Connelly in defence and Kenny Dalglish in attack, for both of them missed only two league matches.

Celtic faced a very real challenge. It was a tribute to their merit that, no matter how narrowly, they overcame it.

So let's look back at the 34 steps that traced a path to more football history.

SEPTEMBER: It all started on a sunny Saturday evening at Hampden. The fixture against Kilmarnock had been switched there because of further reconstruction work to the Parkhead stand.

And because it clashed with a Queens Park match on Saturday afternoon it became an evening kick-off. But, as only 10,000 people watched the game, it was an experiment that was not repeated.

17

18    Challenge . . . between Dixie Deans and Hearts defender
Eddie Thomson in a battle for the ball at Parkhead.

The effectiveness of a sliding tackle . . . as Billy McNeill 19
slides in just in time to take the ball away from the strong-
running Alfie Conn.

Celtic won 6–2, banging their goals past Alistair Hunter, the man who by a twist of football fate was to become their team-mate only four months later.

The scorers were Harry Hood, 3, Dixie Deans, 2, Bobby Murdoch from a penalty and Jackie McGrory own goal.

Then they had a comfortable 2–0 victory against Morton at Cappielow, with two goals from deputy skipper Bobby Murdoch, one of them a penalty.

Two weeks after the opening fixture Celtic were back at Hampden, and still it was not a three o'clock kick-off. This time it was the famous high noon confrontation against Rangers.

It had been decided to start at noon, and also cut the size of the crowd, in a bid to stamp out hooliganism at the 'Old Firm' match.

And before the rest of Britain had started on their diet of Saturday afternoon football Celtic had finished their day's work,

20    Saved on the line . . . Falkirk 'keeper Alistair Donaldson stops this shot from Tommy Callaghan as it seems ready to slip over.

with a crushing 3–1 victory over their old rivals.

Two first-half goals by Kenny Dalglish and Jimmy Johnstone were topped off by Lou Macari in the second half. So few Rangers' fans had waited to see John Greig score for the Ibrox side in the dying minutes of the game that he even got a sympathetic cheer from the Celtic supporters.

Jock Stein had written on the opening day of the league season that his team were after championship number eight, and Celtic had started in double-quick time about going the right way to collect it.

But they received a dull thud when they crashed 2–0 to Dundee at Dens Park, in a game they really did not deserve to win.

However back at Parkhead again for a game marked by the unfurling of the championship flag Dixie Deans gave them a winning end to the month with a 1–0 victory against Ayr United.

Down goes the ref . . . as John Paterson skids on the surface    21
as he attempts to stop a flare-up in the Celtic goal during the
Ibrox 'Old Firm' league game.

22    **The 6,000th up . . . and Bobby Murdoch (extreme right) raises his arm in joy after he had scored the vital goal against Partick Thistle.**

OCTOBER started with another shock. This time it came from Airdrie, who held Celtic to a 1–1 draw, and Bobby Lennox was the man who scored the goal that won a point.

Celtic roared back to form the following week with a crushing 4–0 victory against Partick Thistle, and goals from David Hay, Deans, Lennox and Dalglish.

Then they had to fight to overcome East Fife's boring, defensive tactics in a 3–0 victory at Parkhead, with goals from Hood, Deans and Lennox.

But they finished the month with one of their most impressive victories of the entire season. For in a cracker of a game they beat Aberdeen, the team who had been their closest league rivals for the previous two seasons, by 3–2 at Pittodrie.

Deans and Macari put Celtic quickly ahead by 2–0, but Aberdeen's astute Hungarian, Zoltan Varga, pulled one back before half time. Even when Dalglish made it 3–1 in the second half Varga helped the Dons to a storming finish by scoring a second.

NOVEMBER began with a 3–1 victory against Dundee United at Parkhead, and the goals came from Johnstone, Dalglish and Macari.

And although they were put out of the European Cup by Ujpest Dozsa they slammed back with a 5–0 victory against Motherwell at Fir Park. The scorers were Hood, 2, Dalglish, 2, and McCallum, own goal.

Then they followed up by beating Hearts 4–2 at Parkhead, and the goals came from Dalglish, Deans, Johnstone and Hood.

Just to round off a successful domestic month they came away with two points from Brockville—always a tricky spot for Celtic —with a 3–2 victory when the scorers were Dalglish (2) and Deans.

DECEMBER began with just as much promise. There was a crushing 6–1 victory against Dumbarton at Boghead, when the scorers were Hood, a hat-trick for Pat McCluskey, Johnstone and Cushley, own goal.

The hat-trick was one of only two in the entire league campaign, and they were both against luckless Dumbarton.

They had a week's break in the month for the League Cup Final, but Celtic got back on their winning league way with a 2–1 victory against Arbroath at Gayfield, and both the goals came from Harry Hood.

They had a 1–1 draw against Hibs, then their closest league rivals, in an exciting game at Parkhead and Dalglish was the scorer.

24     Mudlarks . . . as East Fife 'keeper Ernier McGarr and Celtic centre Dixie Deans walk from the Bayview field at the end of the dramatic 2 : 2 clash.

But it was at the end of December that the troubles struck. First manager Jock Stein was taken to hospital with a heart complaint, then as a flu outbreak swept over Britain Celtic had so many players affected that the Scottish League gave them permission to postpone their match against Kilmarnock.

JANUARY . . . started on just as gloomy a note. The New Year fixture against Morton at Parkhead was also postponed because so many of the team were still down with flu.

But enough had recovered sufficiently for the match on 6 January against Rangers at Ibrox. It was a day of drama on and off the park.

Manager Jock Stein listening to the second-half commentary in his hospital bed heard his team equalise. Derek Parlane had put Rangers ahead with a penalty in the first half, when Evan Williams saved the first attempt but the young Ibrox centre sccored with the rebound.

However Dixie Deans equalised, and it seemed to be heading for a certain 1–1 draw until the Celtic defence boobed and

Opposite : The Celt in the sandwich . . . is centre-half Billy    27
McNeil as he goes up for a corner during a game against
Falkirk at Brockville.

Above : Impact . . . between Rangers 'keeper Peter McCloy and
Celtic's Lou Macari in a league clash at Hampden.

Alfie Conn scored a last-minute winner for Rangers to make it 2–1.

But the drama was not over. For minutes after the final whistle assistant manager Sean Fallon, who was in charge of the team, announced that the club had decided to reluctantly agree to a transfer request by Lou Macari and put him on the transfer list.

However a week later, with Jock Stein back watching them from a seat in the directors' box, Celtic defeated Dundee by 2–1, when the scorers were Johnstone and Dalglish.

And a week later they notched up an impressive away victory at Ayr, when in a snow-storm Deans and Dalglish, 2, scored in a 3–1 victory.

But on 27 January the strain was beginning to tell. New keeper Alistair Hunter made his début, but sadly it was not a winning one for Celtic were beaten 2–1 by Airdrie at Broomfield, when Deans scored.

It was an unhappy match. Bobby Murdoch missed a penalty, the points were lost to a last-minute goal by Airdrie, and there were unhappy scenes at the end.

Airdrie, who were later relegated, certainly knew how to take points off Celtic. They had grabbed three out of a possible four in their two meetings.

FEBRUARY brought a brighter start to the league programme with a sparkling 4–0 victory against Kilmarnock at Rugby Park, and two goals from Dalglish, and one each from Johnstone and George Connelly.

But even in this match a penalty miss caused a headache for the next fixture. It came in the last minute when Kenny Dalglish missed a spot-kick that would have been the club's 6,000th league goal.

So the fans had to wait until the following fixture against Partick Thistle at Parkhead. But anxiety gripped Celtic like an octopus, and ran right through the team.

Thistle scored first, and it was only in the second half that Bobby Murdoch scored the equaliser, and goal number 6,000.

Sensibly he worried more about another point dropped when he said after the game: 'Naturally I am pleased to have scored, but I would have been happier if we had won.'

Murdoch was presented with the match ball, and a china tea set by masseur Jim Steele.

A week later came an even bigger shock, when Celtic could only draw 2–2 with East Fife at Bayview, and dropped their sixth league point in seven weeks.

The pressure of an 'Old Firm' match, and it's all shown in this
picture as a crush of players—left to right Billy McNeill,
Sandy Jardine, Jimmy Johnstone, Colin Jackson and Peter
McCloy—surround Rangers goal.

This was one of only three league games played on a day when the weather wiped out almost the entire Scottish calendar. It would have been a sensational result even if everyone had been playing.

Deans had given Celtic a first-half lead, but then East Fife equalised in the second half . . . and Celtic's penalty hoodoo struck.

For they missed the sensational total of three spot-kicks. Murdoch put the first one over the bar, and when the referee ordered it to be re-taken because of a defensive infringement Harry Hood hit the second try at East Fife 'keeper Ernie McGarr.

And Dalglish had miss number three with another penalty after that. East Fife had gone ahead, and it was only three minutes from time that Deans equalised to save Celtic's face, and a 2–2 score.

The month ended on a slightly happier note with a 4–0 win against St. Johnstone at Parkhead, when Lennox (2), Hay and Dalglish scored.

MARCH began with the side showing better form . . . they even scored with a penalty. That was in a 2–0 win against Aberdeen at Parkhead, and Bobby Lennox was the man put

30    Salute from a scorer . . . as Rangers keeper Peter McCloy lies on the ground in despair, Jimmy Johnstone acknowledges the cheers for a goal.

successfully on the spot. Dalglish was the other scorer.

But they had an unimpressive 1–0 win against Morton at Parkhead, one of the New Year postponed fixtures. Paul Wilson played only three league games, but in this match he scored the all-important goal.

And on 10 March Celtic drew 2–2 with Dundee United at Tannadice when Bobby Lennox scored both goals. Now Rangers were neck-and-neck with Celtic, although the champions had an advantage on goal difference.

This was when Celtic showed the real thrust of champions. They had two impressive away victories, a 2–0 win against Hearts at Tynecastle, and Deans and Lennox scored.

They followed that up with a 4–0 win on Grand National Day at a rain-swept Parkhead against Falkirk. The scorers were Deans, Lennox, 2 (one from a penalty) and Hood.

APRIL began a bit shakily and was to end superbly. There was a 2–0 win against Motherwell, with goals from Deans and Dalglish where the points were more impressive than the performance.

Then there was a very good 3–1 victory against St. Johnstone at Muirton, with two goals from Dalglish and one from Jimmy Johnstone.

Fleet-footed Kenny Dalglish zips past an Ibrox guard of Alex MacDonald and Dave Smith to score for Celtic in an 'Old Firm' league game at Hampden.

Now it was coming into the home straight, and poor Dumbarton suffered in a 5–0 defeat at Parkhead. Deans grabbed a hat-trick, Tommy Callaghan and Dalglish were the other scorers.

And four second-half goals against Arbroath at Parkhead— they were scored by Hood, Hay, Deans and Dalglish—finally pushed them ahead.

It was a match marked by cheers from the terraces—at Aberdeen's success against Rangers at Pittodrie. For the fans listened intently on their transistors to hear that Aberdeen had taken a point from the Ibrox side in a 2–2 draw.

The strain of the closest league race for years was shown the next morning with newspaper pictures of the Celtic dug-out even listening to a transistor radio.

So Celtic were ahead again at last. They needed only a draw from their last match against Hibs at Easter Road. They streaked to victory in impressive style with a 3–0 victory.

And it was fitting that the three goals were shared between Dixie Deans and Kenny Dalglish. Deans got two, and Dalglish one.

For between them they scored 45 goals, more than half Celtic's total, and Dalglish just pipped Deans by scoring one more.

It was a memorable way to end a memorable championship win!

# The Struggle for Europe

THE barometer of success has changed out of all recognition in the one hundred years of organised Scottish soccer.

The little group of local footballers returning from some Cup expedition to be hailed by their native village has given way to a new scenario . . . the busy background of an airport.

Celtic were among the first of the teams in Europe engaged in Europe to pioneer, whenever possible, flying back immediately after a game.

The advantages are that players can be in their own homes, only hours after they have travelled across Europe.

And Thursday, normally a day wasted on travelling after the mid-week Wednesday match, can be spent soothing away the rigours of a game abroad.

Sometimes it has meant arriving back at nearly midnight if the team travels on the Wednesday. But if the match has been a victory even that time will not deter the fans turning out in their hundreds for a glimpse of their heroes.

I recall that when the Celtic party arrived late at Abbotsinch after their semi-final aggregate victory over Dukla Prague—and became the first-ever British team to enter the final of the European Cup—a singing and dancing crowd hailed the players on their arrival.

The contrast with their arrival back from another Iron Curtain destination could hardly have been more unhappy.

There were no scarf-waving, singing fans . . . just a small knot of airport workers, a handful of players' wives and a couple of late-duty photographers waiting in the chill of a November night for the team's arrival.

The seventh European Cup campaign had ended dismally only a few hours before on the ground of Ujpest Dozsa, in the Hungarian capital of Budapest.

A season before there had been a different look about the

venue, for then Celtic had beaten the Hungarian team to blast their way gloriously into the European semi-finals.

It had been a sodden pitch that night, with pools of water glistening over part of the surface . . . a surface which would have been difficult for public park players never mind an occasion of the importance of a European tie.

But as the Celtic players had filed happily from their dressing-room that night I remember little Lou Macari looking out at the quagmire and saying with a grin. . . . 'That's the best pitch I have ever played on.'

That night Celtic had won. No one looked happily out on the pitch ten months later . . . it had been the scene of one of Celtic's most bitter nights in Europe.

Perhaps the seeds of the short and not so sweet seventh European campaign had been laid in the first round, when Celtic were drawn against the unrated Rosenburg Trondheim of Norway.

They had earned an easy passage, because they had been semi-finalists the season before, and were seeded for the first-round draw.

Manager Jock Stein had said before the first game—which had been switched to Hampden because of reconstruction at Celtic Park—

'I want to see goals and the foundation laid for a long road in Europe.'

Alas, he was to see neither of his wishes come true.

Certainly Celtic beat Rosenburg 2–1, with goals from Lou Macari and Dixie Deans, but a crowd of only 18,797, created a dreadful lack of atmosphere . . . and the match hardly excited the fans who were there.

Celtic did see enough of the Norwegian 'keeper Geir Karlsen, who played for only a short spell before he was injured, to later offer him a trial at Parkhead; however, it did not work out.

The return match score-line seems comfortable enough, 3–1 for Celtic, on an ice-cold night.

But Celtic still had to negotiate a few problems on their way to the second round on a boggy pitch in front of 15,000 fans.

Rosenburg had equalised, before Macari, Harry Hood and Kenny Dalglish finally pushed Celtic through on a 5–2 aggregate.

Jock Stein remarked before the second-round that he wanted one of Europe's big names as opponents, for he felt his side needed a consistent challenge to give them a cutting edge.

But he added through the propaganda a prophetic remark:

Catch him if you can . . . as the Rosenburg defence chase 35
after Harry Hood in the European game at Hampden.

36    Action time in the Rosenburg goal . . . and this time it's
Lou Macari who is the man firing on target.

A thunderbolt shot from Harry Hood . . . part of Celtic's
barrage on the Rosenburg goal.

Dixie Deans heads the ball towards goal in yet another 37
Celtic attack as the Norwegian defence try to cover.

38    The grim determination of Europe . . . for attackers and defenders. It's all captured in this picture as an Ujpest defender tackles Jimmy Johnstone.

'I said that if we're beaten by the Norwegians we did not deserve to be in the next round . . . and I meant every word of it.'

'If we are beaten, if there are to be headaches and disappointments in Europe this season and our level is only to be in the domestic game then I would rather find it out now.'

He was soon to find out!

Hungarian champions Ujpest Dozsa were the second round opponents, and the Celtic boss paid them the compliment of saying:

'I regard them as technically one of the best teams in Europe. I know because they come from behind the Iron Curtain they lack the solid glamour names such as Cruyff of Ajax or Beckenbauer of Bayern.

'But in my book that does not make them any less dangerous.'

The Celtic manager had privately thought his young team might have been beaten the season before by Ujpest . . . the forecast was to be wrong by nine months.

Imre Kovacs, the boss of Ujpest, had a grim warning for Celtic when his team landed at Glasgow Airport.

For he said: 'We are in a better condition to face Celtic this season, just wait and see.

'We were not at our best last time because our season had just begun after the winter break. That will not be the case this year, now it is different.'

Celtic cleared away doubts about whether or not Jimmy Johnstone would play and they lined up: Williams, Hay, McGrain; Connelly, McNeill, Callaghan; Johnstone, Dalglish, Deans, Macari and Hood.

But they were soon to find out that Ujpest were a different proposition from the team who had played the previous season.

For the purple-clad Hungarians calmly swept into a twenty-minute lead, thanks to veteran striker Ferenc Bene.

And it was only a half-time switch by Celtic which saved the situation. Pat McCluskey was brought on to stiffen the Parkhead defence, which had looked a bit wobbly, and Harry Hood went off.

At the same time sweeper George Connelly was told to move upfield, and within only four minutes the changes worked when Kenny Dalglish grabbed the equaliser.

Now Celtic really put the pressure on Ujpest. But it took a second substitution to work the trick, and put them ahead.

It was a move not too popular with a section of the 55,000 crowd for manager Stein took off Jimmy Johnstone, and brought on Bobby Lennox.

40    Up, up and away above the heads of the Ujpest defence goes Dixie Deans in the European Cup match.

A hustle and bustle in the Ujpest goalmouth as Celtic 41
launch an all-out attack and Lou Macari lies on the ground
as his header sneaks past.

42   That man McNeill again . . . and it's the Celtic skipper in
his old familiar role, helping out his mates in attack as he
dashes up for a corner.

But the jeers which had greeted the decision soon changed, for with his first touch of the ball Lennox crossed for Dalglish to score a second.

However Celtic could not stretch the lead—the life-line they needed for the return trip to Budapest—to more than one goal.

So for the second time in less than a year Celtic set out for the capital city of Hungary on European Cup business.

Budapest was once known as 'the Paris of the East', now it looks as if the whole place could do with a lick of paint.

But there was an Indian summer atmosphere, even although it was the first week in November, before the grim drawbridge of winter was lowered on Eastern Europe.

Certainly it was warm enough for Celtic to sit in shirt-sleeves to watch a U.E.F.A. Cup-tie the day before their own match.

As always with any European match the question-marks swirled about before the game, as much a part of the scene now as the pre-match training.

Celtic's problem was an injury to Lou Macari. He was put through an exhaustive fitness test but was eventually ruled out and so the team was:

Williams, McGrain, Brogan; Hay, McNeill, McCluskey; Johnstone, Connelly, Dalglish, Callaghan, Lennox.

This was the game where Celtic had no chance to even launch the lifeboats, the European hopes for the season foundered totally and without trace in just 20 minutes.

The men who led the destruction were Ujpest's international pair of Ferenc Bene and Anton Dunai, a perfectly-matched football double bill . . . the skills of Bene dove-tailing with the precision of a soccer engineer to the strong running of Dunai.

It states the screamingly obvious to say that the start of a match is a vital time for any team . . . but it has become even more so in these European matches.

The home team, with the benefit of a naturally totally partisan crowd, urges on their team for a quick goal. If an opposing side can hold for that hectic opening half-hour they have a real chance of blunting the initial assault.

It was never to be that way with Celtic. For as the autumn darkness closed in around the trim little tree-lined Ujpest stadium it also swept over the former champions' European hopes.

For inside the first 22 minutes Ujpest had not only gained the vital aggregate equaliser, but had swept into an impregnable 4–2 lead over the two ties, a paid-up insurance to take them into the next round.

43

Jock Stein admitted sadly later: 'We had a dreadful first 20 minutes when we never got together.

'That spell crucified us. I thought if we had got one back in the second-half then we might have had a chance.'

Ujpest let only eight minutes tick by before they snapped the equaliser, when Bene scored after Dunai had beaten McNeill.

Eight minutes later came the second Ujpest goal. George Connelly lost the ball to Zambo ten yards outside the Celtic penalty area.

The winger cut in the box, and with the Celtic defence in a panic, Danny McGrain tackled the outside-left from behind and when he fell Danish referee Bent Neilsen immediately gave a penalty.

Fazekas took the kick, and although 'keeper Evan Williams guessed right and dived to the correct side the ball still beat him and finished low in the corner of the net.

Then in 22 minutes came the final nail in the soccer coffin, when Bene scored his third.

Certainly in the second-half Celtic did tighten up, and played with more style. They even made chances of their own when the keeper touched a Dalglish shot on to the bar, and a McNeill header was cleared off the line.

But really no team in Europe can expect to lose three goals in such a short spell and still hope to survive.

Celtic's agony abroad was no less than the domestic agony of Scottish Television, who had announced special plans to screen the match live from Budapest.

Thousands of fans took the afternoon off work to make sure they would be at home around tea-time to watch the match, and sadly ended up by not seeing a kick of the ball.

The cameras whirred all right, commentator Arthur Montford talked his way through the game, but a fault in the cable line between Budapest and Vienna ruined the entire effort.

Maybe after that dreadful Celtic start to the match it was merciful they were spared a public peep-show of their humiliation.

Celtic took the defeat with dignity and Jock Stein summed it up best when he said: 'We met a team who were better than us on the night, who deserved to win.

'Managers often put up apologies for their side when they lose. I don't think that's necessary this time, not when we were beaten by a better team.

'One of our problems is moving from the comparative safety of the Scottish league to Europe, the difference is the night and

Just in time . . . a foot from an Ujpest defender pokes out 45
to push the ball away from the onrushing Kenny Dalglish.

A tough task for Kenny Dalglish . . . as he tries to take on the
Ujpest defence during the game at Parkhead.

the day.

'But it is something we overcame in the past and we must
do so again.

'Ujpest had players who came good for them at the right time,
notably right-half Toth, who I predict can become one of the
great stars of Europe.

'The Hungarians did a lap of honour after beating Celtic.
That's almost unheard of behind the Iron Curtain, it shows
how highly they rated their victory.'

The official European Union report described ex-champions
Benfica, who were beaten by Derby, and Celtic as the most
eminent 'victims' of the second round.

For Celtic, who had only once before failed to reach the lofty
heights of the quarter-finals in their seven European Cup
campaigns, it was a compliment they did not really want!

# An Unhappy Hat-trick

THE position was the same as they had occupied at two previous League Cup Finals. But sadly for Celtic it was not first up the steps to the Hampden directors' box, and the sight of the League Cup held high to the chanting thousands of fans.

For the third season in succession they had to stand below, in the unhappy position of runners-up, and watch the League Cup slip away from their grasp.

This time the team who had triumphed over them were Hibs, two seasons before it had been Rangers, the season previous it was Partick Thistle.

It had been Celtic's ninth successive final, but a strange hoodoo had wrapped itself round their efforts to win the competition.

No one could say that they were unlucky. Celtic's officials sportingly admitted after the game that Hibs had deserved to win.

And few people would argue that when the final was played Hibs were one of the best teams in the country, producing a brand of football that made them worthy Cup winners.

And it does not detract from Hibs' performance in the final to say that, apart from their showing, the League Cup was the competition football would prefer to forget.

The foundations for its failure were laid in a moment of madness when the clubs made a decision to change the format of the League Cup . . . and many of them were to bitterly regret it.

The tourney had always been one of football's most successful money-spinners. A start of the season boost to the clubs' bank balances, and it was all neatly finished by the end of October.

Maybe the only niggling doubt was that because it was over so quickly the winner's names were sometimes forgotten by the fans by the time April came around.

*Following page:* Celtic's keeper Evan Williams steps smartly    47
to snatch the ball as Hibs centre Alan Gordon dives into the
penalty box.

But it served its purpose well, a bright and brisk competition until the planners got their hands on it.

For the new master-plan meant that the qualifying sections were composed of teams made up from both the First and Second Divisions.

The top two teams from each section would qualify, which meant an additional round for the qualifiers before the quarter-finals.

The clubs must have been nodding to have let the scheme go through, and their cries of pain were soon to be heard.

For while it helped the Second Division teams, with the aid of the First Division sides visiting their grounds, it was disastrous for the gates of the big clubs.

So many fixtures were a mere formality, and the fans, who normally had a keen appetite for matches in the early summer and autumn, stayed away in their thousands.

It was to be a body blow from which Scottish football never truly recovered for the rest of the entire season.

Celtic opened against Stirling Albion at Annfield, and pushed themselves to a comfortable 3–0 victory, with two goals from Lou Macari and Kenny Dalglish.

But the real headlines were not made by the team, they came from their manager!

For at half-time, aften an outbreak of chanting which particularly annoyed him, manager Jock Stein—who was starting to make his way to the dressing-room suddenly turned and closely followed by physiotherapist Bob Rooney made his way on to the terraces.

He jumped into the crowd, and delivered a verbal broadside to the trouble-makers among the fans. It must have made them squirm.

Later he said: 'My action was not a decision made on the spur of the moment. It was something I had wanted to do for a long time, tell the trouble-makers man to man what I thought of their actions.

'I am sure I spoke for the thousands of decent fans who are fed up of having their enjoyment spoiled by the loutish minority.

'I admit I did feel a moment's unease at diving into a packed terrace, but it proved what I have always believed that there are far more good fans than hooligans.'

The competition then continued on its non-eventful way . . . with a 1–1 home draw against East Fife, when Dalglish was the scorer.

Then came a 5–0 win against Arbroath at Gayfield, with a

50    A line-up of Celtic players, but they still cannot stop Pat Stanton putting the ball into the net . . . and Celtic on their way out of the League Cup.

penalty by Bobby Murdoch, two goals from Dalglish and two from Dixie Deans.

They beat East Fife 3–2 at Methil, with Lennox and Dalglish, 2, scoring. And Stirling at home with another 3–0 victory, this time the goals came from Murdoch, Dalglish and Deans.

And with the section already won the only slight tremor of a shock was a 3–3 draw in the final qualifying match against Arbroath, a fixture which was switched from Parkhead to Hampden, because of ground repair work.

The scorers were Cargill, own goal, Hood and Dalglish . . . and the match was watched by Celtic's smallest-ever League Cup crowd, only 5,000 fans.

Then came two matches against Second Division Stranraer, a 2–1 win at Stair Park with goals from Vic Davidson and Lennox, and a 5–2 victory at Parkhead, with the scorers being Lennox, 2, Deans and Murdoch, penalty.

Celtic were now drawn against Dundee in the quarter-finals, a fixture which was played on a home and away basis and took a third game to settle . . . which helped to push up the meetings between the two sides to seven in one season.

And in the League Cup they were packed with controversy on and off the field.

Curiously in the first game Celtic turned on some of their best football of the season, yet still ended the game by losing 1–0 at Dens Park. But it was only a marvellous display of goal-keeping by Dundee's Thomson Allan which robbed them of victory on a night when they displayed much of the fluency which eluded them in other games.

So the stage was set for a soccer spine-tingler in the second game at Celtic Park, and the Scottish League appointed referee Bobby Davidson to both games.

There had been controversy between the club and the referee on past occasions in previous seasons, this game was to write another unhappy chapter.

Celtic equalised on aggregate in 15 minutes with a goal by Bobby Lennox, but then came a controversial Dundee goal when the linesmen seemed to indicate that the ball had crossed the bye-line before it was sent over for Gordon Wallace to score.

However the referee ignored it, just as he rejected pleas from Dundee when they claimed Lou Macari had handled when he scored a second goal for Celtic.

Macari appeared to have wrapped up a semi-final place for Celtic with a third goal before half-time which put them 3–1

52    Battle between two . . . as Hibs sweeper John Blackley and
      Celtic captain Billy McNeill stretch for a corner.

ahead in the match, and on the all-important aggregate count by 3–2.

But Jocky Scott scored a great second-half goal to tie the game on aggregate, and push it into extra time.

It was then that Celtic boss Jock Stein made a move which, on reflection, can only be considered to have been unwise. Obviously annoyed by some of the decisions he went to the middle of the field at the end of ordinary time and appeared to say something to the referee and linesmen.

He was subsequently reported to the SFA by Mr. Davidson, and later fined £100 and and severely censured for that action.

But the extra-time spell proved goal-less, and so the game went to a Hampden replay, but not before there was a new controversy about the referee.

For the Scottish League claimed that Celtic had asked for Mr. Davidson to be withdrawn from the third game, although the club adamantly denied that they had made any such suggestion.

But the verbal duel went on when Celtic director Tom Devlin, a member of the League Management Committee, said: 'A discussion took place about the situation but I can say as Celtic's official representative at the meeting no approach was made to change the referee.'

Fortunately Mr. Davidson did not figure prominently in the proceedings at Hampden, for Celtic swept to an impressive 4–1 victory . . . and all the goals came in the first half, and they were all from headers.

Dundee scored first, that man Jocky Scott again. But the response was quick and decisive for in 27 minutes a Johnstone cross was back-headed by Deans to Harry Hood who nodded the ball into the net.

Then in 35 minutes Kenny Dalglish headed a second and three minutes later crossed the ball for Deans to notch the third headed goal.

And the centre, again with his head, scored the fourth three minutes from half-time to completely knock Dundee out by 4–1.

Celtic's old rivals in the two previous League championships, Aberdeen were their next hurdle in the semi-final.

And on a night when the weather produced a mixture of rain and wind Celtic triumphed by 3–2, even although they trailed twice in the game.

Joe Harper (later transferred to Everton) had always been a danger man to Celtic and he proved it aagin by scoring in 30 minutes, but three minutes later when Dalglish was pulled down

56    *Previous page:* The final nail in Celtic's League Cup Final coffin . . . as Hibs Jimmy O'Rourke heads his side's second goal.

Celtic's only moment of joy in the League Cup Final, as Kenny Dalglish slots the ball past Hibs keeper Jim Herriot.

by Aberdeen left-back Jim Hermiston Celtic equalised with a penalty by Harry Hood.

However Dave Robb put Aberdeen ahead again in the second-half, but seconds later after a move by Brogan and McCluskey Celts again equalised through Jimmy Johnstone.

And with ten minutes to go they scored the all-important third goal, thanks to Tommy Callaghan.

But their League Cup joy ended there, killed by two second-half goals by Hibs which floored Celtic.

The teams had lined up: Williams, McGrain, Brogan; McCluskey, McNeill, Hay; Johnstone, Connelly, Dalglish, Hood, Macari . . . sub, Callaghan.

Hibs: Herriot, Brownlie, Schaedler; Stanton, Black, Blackley; Edwards, O'Rourke, Gordon, Cropley, Duncan . . . sub, Hamilton.

It was to be sweet revenge for Hibs' 6-1 Cup Final drubbing only seven months before. For Stanton and O'Rourke scored in the second-half and although Kenny Dalglish pulled one back for Celtic they could not get the life-line of an equaliser, and the game ended in a 2-1 victory for Hibs.

The League Cup, which at one time had seemed such a permanent fixture at Parkhead that it was only taken to Hampden once a year to be dusted and brought back again, had found a new home yet again!

57

# My pal Jimmy Johnstone

## by BOBBY LENNOX

I DON'T suppose there is any player in Scottish football who is more controversial than Jimmy Johnstone.

Some people idolise him, some are exasperated by him. I know him not just as Jimmy Johnstone who has been a teammate of mine for over ten years . . . but as the person who has been my best friend at Celtic Park for all that time.

What makes him tick, and what are the flaws that sometimes afflict the play of the little red-headed right winger?

I think you have to start by saying that he's like any great player—and to me wee Jimmy is a great player—and he's a bit temperamental.

That touch of temperament is something that goes with any great player, as much a part of their equipment as their boot laces.

Yet, more than any other player in Scotland, I believe he gets more pressure put on him from opposing players. And to me he has one skill above all his others . . . and it's the one which has probably let him keep playing football.

That is his brilliant ability to ride a tackle. People say George Best is a stronger player, and they point out how he can tackle better than other wingers.

But defenders whack Jimmy at times in tackles, and attempted tackles, and he just bounces back. I reckon the fact that he does not get many injuries considering the sort of treatment he receives is a massive tribute to his strength.

And he's not a player who fakes injuries—something I cannot stand in football—for when he's down he wants back up to get on with the game.

I have three vivid memories of Johnstone at his best. One of them was against Red Star of Belgrade in a European Cup game at Parkhead when we beat them 5–1, and he was truly fantastic.

The other was a league game against Dundee United at Park-

Bobby Lennox . . . as the ball blurs its way from that lethal left foot towards goal in a game against Falkirk.

head when we scored seven against them, and as I was a spectator that night I could sit back in a stand seat and really appreciate him.

The third occasion was against Real Madrid in Spain for Alfredo Di Stefano's benefit match, which was played just after we had won the European Cup.

I have a mental picture forever etched in my mind of wee Jimmy standing with the ball about seven yards from a defender, and baffling him by just dropping his shoulder.

It's a trick of his—I swear he does it even if you are walking down the street with him—and that night the crowd in the Bernabeau Stadium literally rose on their feet to applaud him.

Crowd atmosphere affects the wee man. If it's a big game I think he pulls out an extra effort to provide entertainment.

60       A moment away from the cares of football for Bobby Lennox, as he walks on the beach near his Ayrshire home with daughter Gillian, son Gary . . . and not forgetting Rebel the dog.

His value to his team-mates is that if you are in a tight-spot you can always give it to Jimmy.

I suppose the players are like the fans, we feel that if he has the ball something is going to happen.

I know there has often been controversy between Jimmy and the club, but that is not a matter which concerns me here. I am speaking of him as a friend, and I consider him a person who would do anything to help his friends.

The fact is that Jimmy and I grew up together, along with players such as Tommy Gemmell and Bobby Murdoch, and we played together for a few seasons in the reserve side.

I was shown a 1961 newspaper cutting recently which named three bright youngsters who were provisionally signed by Celtic, and from whom the club were expecting great things . . . they were Robert Lennox of Ardeer Rec, Tom Gemmell of Coltness United and James Johnstone of Blantyre Celtic.

Actually our spell in the reserve team was like an apprenticeship. Boys now tend to come into teams straight from school in some sides.

This does not happen at Celtic, but it does with other clubs, and I think it puts an added strain on the kids.

Both Jimmy and myself are pretty keen followers of the pops charts, and it helped us on that marvellous day of the European Cup final when we played Inter-Milan in Lisbon.

It was a very long walk from the dressing-rooms to the pitch, so we started singing . . . I think we had just about completed the number by the time we arrived at the field.

I am very proud to have been a member of that European Cup-winning team. Players from all over Britain had tried for so long to conquer Europe . . . it was a wonderful honour to have been a member of the team who finally achieved the breakthrough.

I have always believed that the basis for success of that European Cup campaign was the five-week close-season tour we made of America.

We had never been together for so long. We played all kinds of opposition, from matches against Spurs and Bayern Munich to local opposition . . . and we were undefeated.

But the major advantage was that we hammered out a playing formula that was to take us to European glory.

For me the strength of that European Cup-winning side was in its backbone. If you looked down the spine of the side we had experience where it mattered.

We had Ronnie Simpson in goal, Billy McNeill in the middle

*Following page:* It's a hit and a miss . . . a hit for Bobby    61
Lennox as he scored with a spot-kick against Falkirk, and a
miss for the photographer who seems to have lost the
Brockville goalkeeper.

Flashback . . . to one of the great moments in the career of
Bobby Lennox, as airport workers welcome him back at
Glasgow, along with Scotland team-mates Willie Wallace
(left) and Billie Bremner (centre) after the 3:2 victory
against England at Wembley in 1967.

of the defence, Bertie Auld in mid-field and Stevie Chalmers and
Willie Wallace in the centre of the attack.

The rest of us were a bit younger so we could all run about—
I better not say they did not run about or they will rise from
their wheel-chairs to clobber me—but that blend of experience
was the lynch-pin of the side.

We all wanted to play for each other as well. If someone hit
a long ball upfield there would always be at least one player
who would chase it to try to create even a half-chance.

I don't think anyone was jealous of anyone else. I played
number 10 or 11 at the time, and if I was left-winger that
usually meant John Hughes would be left out the team.

But he would be right into the dressing-room to shake my
hand and say 'all the best, wee man—do your stuff'. Everyone
was the same, it happened on the other wing when sometimes

64    A warning for Bobby Lennox, and Rangers centre-half
Ron McKinnon as referee Bill Anderson tries to quieten
things down during a tense moment in an 'Old Firm' game.

Willie Wallace—or 'Wispie' as we called him—would take over from wee Jimmy.

You cannot live on memories in football, but I do look back with a special nostalgia to 1967.

Principally, of course, for the European Cup. But also because that year I was in the Scottish team which beat England 3–2 at Wembley . . . the first defeat for them after winning the World Cup.

Teams can be planned for months or years, but sometimes— maybe without all that much effort—everything clicks . . . and that's what happened in 1967.

There were some really great names in that team, and I have never known the Anglos in the team so determined to win.

66    The inseparables off the park . . . Jimmy Johnstone (extreme right) and Bobby Lennox share a coffee table with Dixie Deans (left) and Lou Macari before Celtic set off on a Continental flight.

Don't let anyone kid you that just because a player is transferred to England he still loses sight of the fact that he is a Scot. I think if it's possible they were more desperate than the home Scots for a victory.

Because England won the World Cup they had to put up with so much stick from their team-mates in the various clubs that they were really bursting for a win.

We went to Wembley for the usual look-around on the Friday before the game, and the big score-board naturally registered o–o.

I was standing next to Chelsea's Eddie McCreadie, who was then our left-back. He turned to me and said: 'If that's the score tomorrow I'm going into Stamford Bridge on Monday with my Scottish strip on.'

As we went one better and beat England I often wonder if he did it!

I still bear the scars of that game, for I have a trace of stud marks on my knee caused by a tackle by England centre-half Jackie Charlton.

Frankly I was lucky to escape without a serious injury. Billy Bremner has since told me that they have a photograph of the incident at Leeds.

It shows Charlton's boot making contact with my knee and I should have come out of it with a shattered knee cap.

But instead it was the big Leeds man who came off worse, for by a lucky freak for me there was a flaw in one of his studs. It cracked, and went up through his boot and broke his toe.

But the film of the game sometimes makes me feel my age. It was before the four-step rule for goalkeepers was introduced, and it shows Ronnie Simpson—Scotland's keeper that day— charging about with the ball on the eighteen yard line.

1967 also reminds me of one of the blackest moments in Celtic's history, the ill-fated World Club championship match with Racing Club of Argentine . . . and I was one of the players ordered off, the only time in my career I have ever been sent off.

In fact, the only previous time I had been in trouble with a referee was a booking I once got in a reserve match.

I remember in that play-off match in Montevideo as I trudged off Mr. Stein could not believe it. He shouted at me that there must have been some mistake and to get back on the park.

And again I was sent off. It turned out, for some reason to which only the ref. knows the answer, that just before he had warned Billy McNeill that the next tackle he considered illegal from our No. 6 or No. 8 would result in a sending off . . . and I just happened to be No. 8 that day.

*Following page:* The Parkhead pair of Bobby Lennox and
Jimmy Johnstone together again . . . as Lennox appeals
for a goal when Johnstone beats Aberdeen goalkeeper
Bobby Clark in a Scottish Cup-tie at Parkhead, but it was
disallowed for offside.

I am afraid it illustrates the farce to which the level of the game had fallen, but at least I was exonerated when the S.F.A. Referee Committee finally investigated the whole unhappy affair.

When I was younger I thought 29 or 30 was old. I really did look on it that way when I was around 21. Now of course I've changed my outlook, for I feel as fit as ever.

I've always tried to keep myself fit. You get trained hard at Celtic Park anyway, but if I don't play on a Saturday, I tend to go out by myself on a Sunday.

And I still like to score goals. It all depends on how the gaffer says you have got to play. If Mr. Stein says you've got to play wide on the wing then there's obviously not a lot of chances to score from there.

I don't find it difficult to adapt from one role to another. Mr. Stein says how we play, and we all try to follow. Anyway, I've grown up with the gaffer, I didn't start playing with the team until he came.

It's nice to be in a pool of players getting money. But I admit that it's nice to see your name in the papers, there's a wee bit of glory attached to it.

I've been fortunate at times when I've been playing badly, and maybe sticking a goal in. That's probably luck as much as anything else.

Like all goal-scorers I tend to remember the ones that got away, just as much as the ones I scored. And top of my list of goals that did not count was the last-minute score I notched against Liverpool at Anfield in the 1966 European Cup-Winners Cup semi-final.

That was chalked off for offside, although two Liverpool defenders, left-back Gerry Byrne and goalkeeper Tommy Lawrence both agreed there was nothing wrong with it.

And, of course, that disallowed goal would have been good enough to have taken us through to the final.

I suppose the modern image of footballers has changed a great deal from when I started first of all. Now the public seem to think it's a constant whirl of birds, boutiques and booze.

But I would like to try to straighten the record a bit. Frankly a big night out for me is a night at the pictures.

I'm a great TV fiend, and it would take an earthquake or a game to move me from the telly on a Monday night and my favourite Western 'Alias Smith and Jones'.

I've even got two TV sets in the house. Because I stay on the Ayrshire coast it means I can pick up the national TV sports shows which are beamed to Ulster, and watch the Scottish ones at the same time.

It's well worth it . . . especially if I can see Celtic scoring on two different programmes at the same time!

# The Best Job in the Team

## by GEORGE CONNELLY

THE scoring chances of a striker . . . the swooping dives of a 'keeper . . . the darting touch-line dribbles of a winger.

I know these are the glamour positions that kids kicking a football in back streets dream about, these are the positions from which players make headlines.

But I want to make a plea for the position in which I play . . . the one that I think is the best in the team, the sweeper.

I suppose if you had mentioned the word sweeper fifteen years ago most people would have thought you were talking about cleaning carpets.

But, with the numbers game that revolutionised tactics in the fifties and the sixties came the new position of sweeper, the man who plays behind or alongside the centre-half.

People are beginning to notice the position. The 'sweeper's club' have cornered the market in Scotland's 'Player of the Year' title for the last three seasons.

Martin Buchan won it when he was with Aberdeen, Dave Smith of Rangers followed him and then I had the honour to win it after him.

And Bobby Moore has raised the position to a fine football art during his time as skipper of England and West Ham.

I must admit I did not start my career with the thought that I would fill the number six position myself.

I was an inside-right when I first went to Celtic, I had spells on the wing with them and at one time I thought I would eventually finish up as a centre-half.

But now I reckon that sweeper is the best position for me. And while I have a tremendous admiration for Bobby Moore I don't copy his style for the England skipper really does very little attacking in his position, he's quite happy to mop everything up and stay at the back.

I must admit that if the chance is on I like a gallop upfield

The authority of George Connelly . . . as he appeals to Celtic     73
fans to stop throwing missiles in the tense moments as
Jimmy Johnstone, escorted by Bobby Murdoch, is sent off
during the game against Aberdeen.

from time to time. For frankly I think sweeper can be turned into a very lazy position.

It's easy enough to tuck yourself in at the back, and not advance over the eighteen yard line for eighty minutes.

But, as I say, I aim to do a wee bit of attacking and it suits me fine. I feel I am an asset to the team in the sweeper position.

Yet I don't know whether I will stay there, for I have learned that the one thing you cannot do in football is look too far ahead.

I got to know that very quickly, when I had two offers to turn senior. One came from Celtic, and one came from Dunfermline, then managed by a certain Mr. Jock Stein.

I remember the night he came to my home. I had already fixed up to travel to Celtic Park the next night and he told me I should keep that appointment.

But he also gave me the run-down on how things would work if I went to Dunfermline. Even then the force of the man came through, although I was only a 14-year-old boy at the time.

So I went to Parkhead the next night and to be honest I was a wee bit over-awed by the whole place, and if it had been left to me I don't know that I would have agreed to sign.

However I took the advice of my father and did join Celtic. I knew Mr. Stein was coming back the next night to my home to find out my decision. But I did not stay in to tell him, I went for a walk rather than say that I would not be joining Dunfermline.

That would have seemed to be the end of any chance of a football partnership with George Connelly and Jock Stein, and there seemed even less hope when he moved to Hibs.

Eventually he did arrive back at Celtic Park, and although I was only one of the ground staff boys, I felt that everything would shoot up after that!

Boys at Parkhead are not pushed into the first team quickly the way they are at some other clubs and while it can some-times cause a bit of frustration I look back now and I am grateful for the soccer education I have been given.

One of the great moments is when you are given the chance of going with the first team on a foreign trip.

There is no chance you will play, you are there to help to carry the hamper and do the chores. However, all the time you are absorbing just what it's like to play abroad, the change in the atmosphere, and the giant differences between playing in a Scottish match and one on the Continent.

One of my greatest experiences—if not one of the happiest for the club—was to go with the team when they travelled to

*Previous page:* Sign, please . . . and George Connelly obliges for a young fan as he comes out of Parkhead, at the same time as manager Jock Stein is going in.

Congratulations . . . to George Connelly from his two-year-old daughter Sharon at the good news that her daddy has just been voted 'Player of the Year'.

South America for the second leg of the ill-fated world championship match against Racing Club of Buenos Aires.

I was brought into the team gradually. I grew so fast my height actually outgrew my strength, and so when I was a bit of a bean-pole I still had spells on the wing.

Maybe the most memorable was when I was deputising for Jimmy Johnstone and was fortunate enough to score against Rangers in a 4–0 Scottish Cup Final victory.

I had actually made my début a good deal earlier, in 1965 during the European Cup-Winners Cup game against Dynamo Kiev.

I suppose it was a bit unique, for I had the stage to myself. I was pretty good at ball-juggling then, my 'keepy-up' average was about 2,000 non-stop, so Mr. Stein decided I should entertain the fans at half-time.

I must admit I was so scared at the thought that when I was standing in the tunnel waiting to go on the park I almost decided to call it off.

But I did go on, and simply went through the routine that I had practised so often in the back-garden of my own home with my four brothers.

It was a long way from that first appearance to a regular place in the first team, and although I was in the pool of players from which the top team was selected it was really only in season 1971–72—the year we made history by winning the seventh championship—that I got a regular place as sweeper and I felt that, at last, I had achieved my breakthrough position.

I suppose I am really part of the new Celtic, the players who were drafted in to take the place eventually of that marvellous European-Cup winning side.

I am sure the fans will remember that Lisbon team for ever, and for what they did for Celtic and Scotland that is only right.

But I think gradually in a few more years they will stop comparing every new player who comes into the side with the men who filled that position in the Lisbon team.

The new players will have worked to make their names in the side, and that's the way it has always been in football.

It was a phenomenal feat to win the European Cup. I've great memories of that side, but you can't live on memories.

That's why the players of today's team are just as anxious to go

80

on to win as much as possible for the club.

The great secret of the eight championship successes is that although the same club has won the honour, it's not been the same team.

So the new players who have slotted in season by season are just as anxious to keep going as the ones who have already won the honours.

And I know that attitude will be passed on to the youngsters who follow us . . . it will be up to them to aim for such a high standard.

They will have to adjust, as we all had to do, to the various aspects of life as a Celtic player. Some of them you get used to, some are always that bit difficult.

Part of it is that you are usually recognised anywhere you go, in restaurants, or—maybe it's because I am tall—certainly by kids if I go shopping with my wife in a supermarket.

I must admit it's not something I enjoy an awful lot. I suppose I've always been a bit shy about that side of the business.

But I realise my responsibilities. I recently moved my home from Fife, where I was born, to live nearer Glasgow to cut out the travelling time every day.

The World Cup would be a great chance to test my soccer philosophy. For I believe you should try to play football all the time.

It may seem a bit corny in an age when so much is at stake, when so often for too many clubs it is win at all costs.

I like winning too. But I believe if you stop trying to play football there is nothing left . . . it is just another game and not something special.

I think players who get in bother with referees in many cases deserve it. I reckon you should get on with your game, and let the ref. get on with his.

Of course it will never always work out that way. There's the human element, but it's something worth striving for in the game . . . it certainly would not be any worse for the trying of it!

# My Dream Move

## by ALISTAIR HUNTER

I'M GLAD that the police did not have a radar trap on the Glasgow-Kilmarnock road one night last January . . . for I reckon I must have broken a few speed limits.

I was on my way to Rugby Park— and I wanted there as quickly as possible—for I had just heard that afternoon that I had the chance to sign for Celtic.

The first hint of a move for me came in an afternoon call from Kilmarnock manager Walter McCrae to the accountant's office in Glasgow where I worked.

He asked me if I was interested in a transfer. And I immediately agreed, although at that stage he did not specify the club, but merely said that a certain side had made me an offer.

The fact was that I was ready to go anywhere. I had nothing against Kilmarnock, but I felt my career had got into a rut, and a move was the best answer.

I had been with the Scotland party in Brazil the previous summer, and when I got back I found it hard to concentrate again with Kilmarnock.

I had been dropped into the reserves, but I felt I had to concentrate on full-time football, and this was obviously my chance.

Fifteen minutes later Mr. McCrae phoned me back to say that the club who wanted me were Celtic . . . and I could not get in my car quick enough.

I had heard so many times over the previous few seasons that Celtic were supposed to be interested in me.

It's the kind of gossip that goes on all the time in football, and when nothing continued to happen I got to the stage that I just shrugged my shoulders whenever anyone mentioned it and I used to think 'here we go again'.

But amazingly this time it was for real. And it took me only ten minutes to sign once I had met Celtic manager Jock Stein

84      What a sad start for Alistair Hunter . . . as he loses one of the goals in his debut for Celtic which gave Airdrie a shock win at Broomfield.

and assistant manager Sean Fallon at Rugby Park.

Celtic are a club I have always wanted to play for, I think that any player naturally wants to have a chance at the top . . . and they have proved they are in that position!

However the fact is that if Rangers had followed up an interest in me I might have been playing for the other half of the 'Old Firm'.

When I was with my youth team, Drumchapel Amateurs, they got a call one day that Rangers were short of a goalkeeper for a third team fixture . . . so I was sent along to fill in.

We played Queens Park at the Albion training ground, and won 5-2. I thought one of the Ibrox officials might have spoken to me at the end, but I was given the cold-shoulder.

I got dressed, collected my gear, went out to have a look at the Ibrox pitch, then went home . . . and I have still to talk to anyone.

It was my first impression of having a trial with a senior club, and after the way I had been ignored I was not impressed by it.

But maybe I had the last laugh. For a few weeks later Rangers had a scout at one of Drumchapel's games and after it Davie White, who was then manager of Rangers, phoned the Drumchapel officials to ask details about me.

They did not seem to know that I had already played with them . . . but I am afraid my experience had put me right off Ibrox altogether.

Perhaps I was fated to have ill-luck with trials, for when I went to England for a week with Leicester City I ran into fixture problems with them.

They were involved in an F.A. Cup quarter-final replay, and a semi-final all squeezed into that week.

Frank O'Farrell, the man who later went to Manchester United, was the boss then but he did not have time to see me play, and it turned out to be a bit of a wasted week.

I did have the chance to turn senior from my junior club, Johnstone Burgh, a year before I eventually moved to Kilmarnock.

But I held off, for frankly I was a bit doubtful about senior football as a career. I had seen a lot of people jump in at the first offer that came to them, and it had backfired.

Perhaps I was a canny accountant, but I thought I had better keep both jobs going. Eventually after I signed for Kilmarnock, I found the schedule of a full-time job and part-time football almost killing.

I used to finish work at five o'clock, and start training just

86 It's a 'no entry' sign, but it could be the emblem of goalkeepers everywhere . . . and certainly of Celtic's new signing, Alastair Hunter.

88    An old Celt and a new one clash . . . and this time it's success
for Alistair Hunter as he pushes a shot from Dave Cattenach,
now with Falkirk, round the post in a league game at
Parkhead.

after six. I don't know whether I was more exhausted mentally or physically at the end of it.

There is just no comparison between the set-up and the preparations of a part-time and a full-time side.

When I was at Kilmarnock I was fortunate enough to find a way into the Scotland set-up, and my first honour was an Under-23 cap against Wales at Swansea.

The international team manager at that time was Bobby Brown. He was a very pleasant person, but he puzzled the team a bit at the pre-match talk when he said we would play in a 4-4-3 formation . . . as an ex-goalkeeper I wondered where he intended to fit me in.

He was followed by Tommy Docherty, a completely different character, and I had a chance to study him, especially on the close-season trip to Brazil.

90    Thumbs up . . . from Celtic's new keeper Alistair Hunter on the day he moved from Kilmarnock to Parkhead.

I suppose he is the most controversial team manager Scotland
has ever had, and some people loathed him just as much as others
liked him.

I know where I stand. Put me down as a fan of the Doc's.
Certainly he's very flamboyant, and the team talks used to have as
many jokes as a Morecambe and Wise script.

But he definitely knew how to lift players. And he had a
serious side to him as well.

I remember at an Under-23 fixture against England at Derby.
I was really nervous in the dressing-room before the match.
He took the time to have a bit of a natter with me, and calmed
me completely.

He made players feel that Scotland were going somewhere.

Even footballers have to do ordinary chores sometimes, and    91
it's time from keeping goal for Alistair Hunter to clean his car.

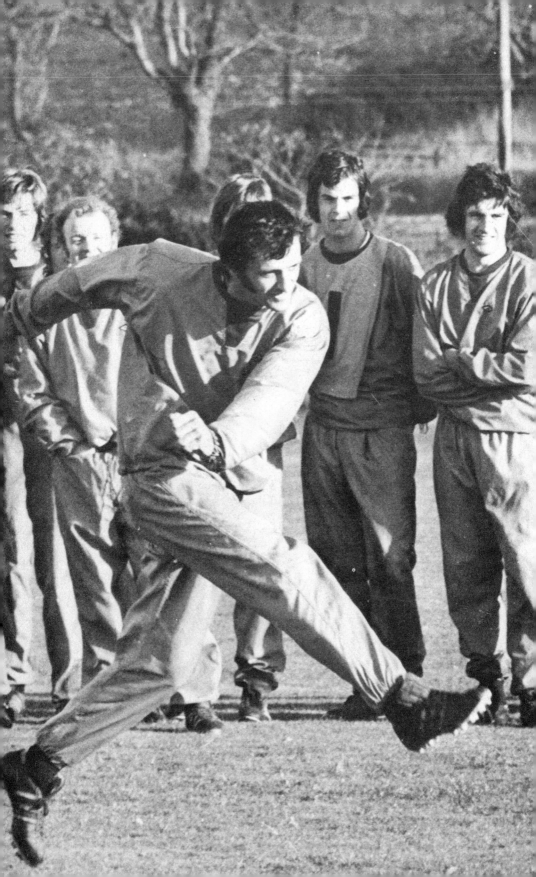

He liked the big time, but he treated the big names just the same as the rest of us, and we all got the idea that we were no longer the country cousins of the international circuit . . . I was really impressed with him.

He certainly managed to keep team spirit going. Perhaps it was because it was so far away but I don't think he ever got the credit for what he achieved with Scotland's side in the Brazilian tournament.

I think he was the only person among the officials who really believed with all his heart that we should make the trip, and when we got there he worked like anything to make sure it succeeded.

Certainly he knew the names of the players, and that was not always the case with the officials. One of them said to me: 'What's your name again?,' and another constantly mixed up Eddie Colquhoun and George Graham.

I am sure I was not the only player who was sorry when the Doc decided to quit Scotland for Manchester United.

When I was in Brazil the other keeper on the tour, Bobby Clark of Aberdeen, and I used to talk about what it would be like to be Celtic's keeper.

Both of us admired Ronnie Simpson tremendously because he coped so well with the special problems which a keeper has at Parkhead.

These are really caused because the team's tactics are always geared to attack, and sometimes it can be as much as ten minutes before their keeper even touches the ball.

But ask any goalkeeper. He likes to get the feel of the ball early on . . . even make a save to get his eye in.

That's not always possible. So I have devised a pre-match schedule in the dressing-room to try to overcome these problems.

Ten minutes before the start of the game I find a quiet corner in the dressing-room, and put myself through a series of loosening-up exercises.

It means that I am alert whenever I go out onto the park, even if I am not called into action immediately.

Ronnie Simpson, by the fact that he was such a great goal-keeper, has also unwittingly caused a few headaches for the men who have followed him.

It's inevitable that Celtic fans always compare the current

94

keeper to Ronnie, but I realised very early that there was no use worrying about it.

I take the view that the job is mine now if I show the right form, and I must work on it from there.

Certainly I am put under pressure at training sessions by our manager. I'm told it's part of the torture treatment he has dreamed up ever since Ronnie Simpson was in goal.

But seriously I think it's marvellous. It sharpens me up tremendously, and sometimes I make more saves at these practice matches than I do in an entire match.

I reckoned from the start that if I was to be boss in the six-yards box I would have to shout right away, even although all my mates were a bunch of international stars.

I'm happy to say that the formula seems to have worked. I don't look on myself now as an outsider keeping goal, but as part of the defensive set-up.

Another aspect that has really helped to sharpen up my game has been crowd atmosphere. It's something you are never without with Celtic, and something that we rarely encountered at Kilmarnock.

I enjoy playing in front of big crowds. When you have been in games where there are so few fans that you can spot the same one on the same section of the terraces every week you welcome any kind of atmosphere.

But most of all in the new season I am looking forward to going into Europe. Kilmarnock had a proud record in the Continental competitions in the mid-sixties.

Sadly I joined them too late to share in it. I try to keep it quiet, but the only tie I played in was probably their worst-ever result . . . when we were beaten in the Fairs Cup by Irish league side, Coleraine.

I hope I can make up for that!

# The Stars of Tomorrow

FEW CLUBS could advertise for a single player . . . and receive 1,500 replies. Yet that's what happened when Celtic Boys' Club put a small advert in a newspaper saying that they wanted a new outside-right.

And the fantastic response of such a deluge of mail symbolises the astonishing rise of a side who in seven years from their origins as a street side in the Maryhill district of Glasgow have now become one of Scotland's premier youth teams.

There is a close link between the Celtic Football Club, and their soccer 'baby brothers'. Although the S.F.A. rules forbid Celtic to sponsor the club completely there are many ways in which a helping hand is given to the Boys' Club.

And now the Boys' Club have moved firmly into another phase of their operation . . . to provide the senior club with a steady conveyor belt of promising youngsters.

The mastermind of the Boys' Club, 25-year-old general manager Jim Torbett, explained to me: 'We are a nursery club for Celtic. There is no doubt about that.

'But it's only over the last couple of years that we have started producing the goods that Celtic require.

'It's taken us five years to get to the standards of play which Celtic want.'

And Torbett's honest assessment of the situation explains why, although they have been going since 1966—and a 16-year-old then would be a mature player of 23 by now—no boy has yet graduated to the Celtic league team from the Boys' Club.

But now the floodgates seem ready to open, and within the next decade a majority of first-team players may be able to proudly proclaim that they started their careers with the Boys' Club.

In the last two years a total of 23 starlets from the Boys' Club have become attached to the senior side, either on an 'S' form—

Following page . . . A V.I.P. line-up for one of the Celtic Boys' Club presentations, with back row (left to right) . . . ex-Celt Joe McBride, manager Jock Stein and players David Hay and Billy McNeill.

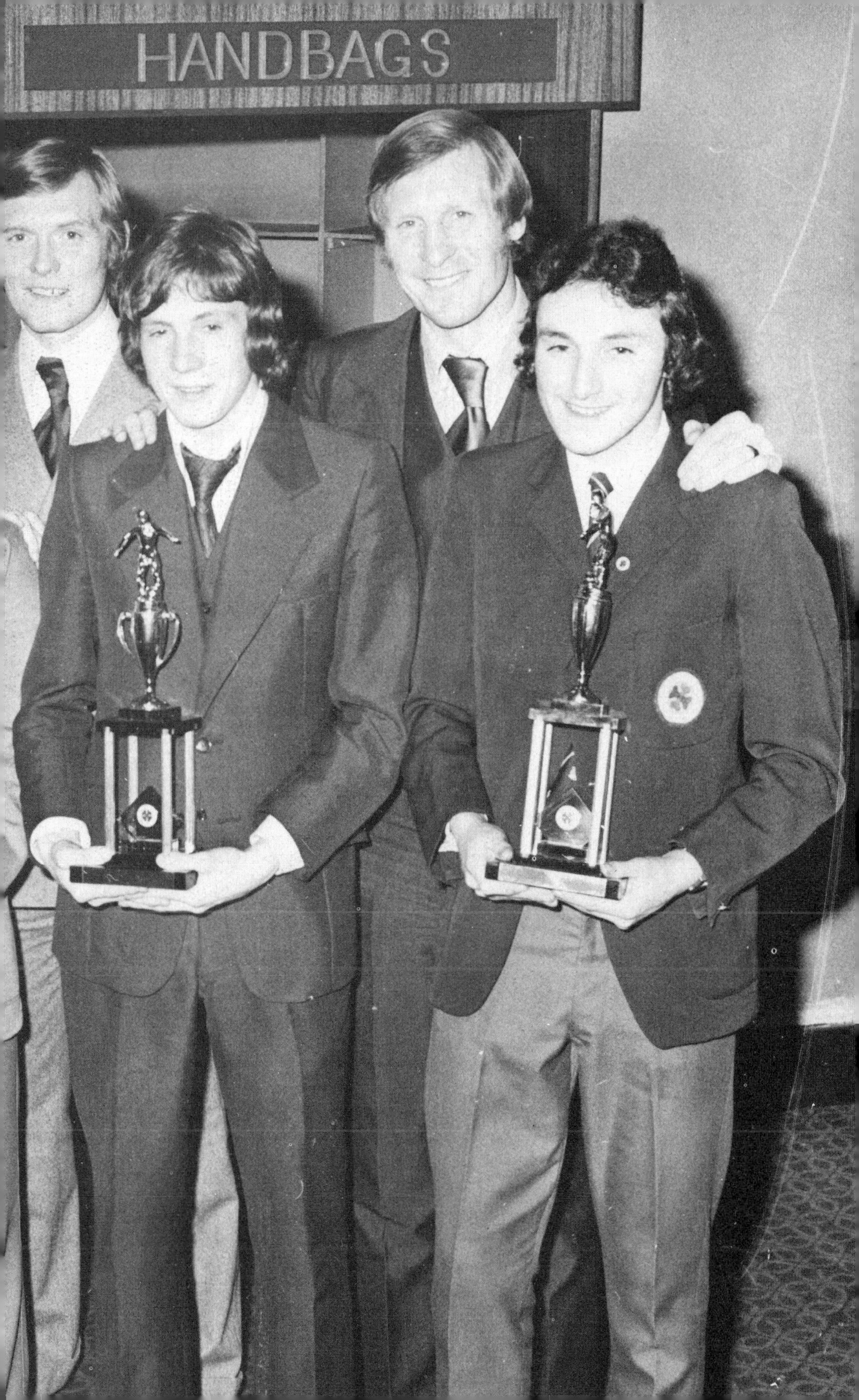
HANDBAGS

the system where clubs can sign under-age players—or as ground staff employees, the traditional stepping stone to stardom.

Jim Torbett looks even farther into the future and says: 'It would be wonderful if one day five or six of the Scotland international side could say they started their career with us.

'The way it is heading just how many of the players at Celtic Park will come from the Boys' Club.

'It has taken us these years to establish ourselves. We had to plug away until we got to the standard that the senior club needed, now it has all been worthwhile.'

The first player to achieve the momentous breakthrough for the Boys' Club could be striker Andy Ritchie, now on the Celtic staff, and already part of Scotland's professional youth international squad.

That would be the culmination of a long road started in the middle sixties when the Celtic Boys' Club was born from a street team called the Mount Youth Side.

Someone suggested that the new team should be called the Celtic Boys' Club, and Jim Torbett got in touch with the then Celtic chairman, Sir Robert Kelly, to ask for official approval.

Later the organisers were invited to Parkhead to meet manager Jock Stein and in Torbett's words 'They sort of adopted us after that'.

It was an adoption which was recognised when the Celtic manager was honoured recently with a special presentation from the Boys' Club.

And in fact one of the early teams had the manager's son, George Stein, in their line-up, although he later quit playing because of his studies.

The enthusiasm which was to fire the club to take trips out of Scotland, to show boys the European soccer scene which even little more than ten years previously had still been so remote, was evident right from the start.

They went to Nantes in the autumn of 1966 to see Celtic start successfully against the French champions on the road which was to lead that season finally to Lisbon.

They also found out early on that the magic name of Celtic brought them recognition abroad which might have taken longer to establish if they had played under some other name.

At one game in Lloret de Mar in Spain they played before a gates-closed crowd of 14,000.

They have been to Germany, Iceland, Spain, twice, and Italy, Holland and Belgium, as well as a tour to Canada and America in 1970, the highlight of all their trips.

100

They were away for five weeks, and in one journey to Toronto they had to overcome the twin problems of heat exhaustion and a punishing schedule of five games in one day to win a tourney . . . which they did!

And their 1973 travel schedule included trips to Switzerland, Sweden and **Portugal.**

I wondered how they managed to raise money for such trips, a far cry from the days when a trip down the Clyde coast might have been considered an adventure for previous generations of budding soccer stars.

Jim Torbett explained: 'We've always been a working club. By that I mean we've got to go out and raise it.

'We believe in making the boys work at fund-gathering, and we only get subsidised from various directions to the amount that has been raised by the lads themselves.

'Then we look around for various ways to get the fare down as cheaply as possible.'

The club started with premises in an old church hall in Maryhill, but they were forced to vacate them when it was burned down.

Then they moved to the car park in front of the main Parkhead stand, but they finally arrived at their present home when Jock Stein appeared one day and said to an astonished and delighted Jim Torbett . . . 'There's the keys of Barrowfield, away and use it'.

And so they have used the Celtic training ground ever since for their activities, which includes running six football teams.

While the main concern is football they have other activities which, although naturally they do not receive their share of the publicity spotlight, are important to the club.

Jim Torbett says: 'We try to encourage the boys to have another hobby as well as football to help broaden their interests.

'We have art competitions. We take them canoeing and fishing. Our captain of the Under-15 side, Kenny Innes, won the last art competition we organised.

'We've also had a successful quiz team in a competition organised by the Glasgow area of youth clubs.

'Obviously our main interest is football. We're geared up for that, but we try through the winter, especially when it's a bit quiet, to get the boys involved in other interests.'

But, of course, football has been the foundation of the club's existence. They could hardly better their 1973 record when all their teams, starting with the Under-12s up to the Under-18s— that's six in all because they do not have an Under-17 side—won

Following page . . . A happy ending to a football flare-up    101
. . . officials and players of Italian side, Santos, present a
pennant to Celtic Boys' general manager Jim Torbett after
an incident during the European youth tournament.

their respective league championships.

And the Under-16 side won their section of the European Youth tournament which was played last Easter and jointly organised by the Boys' Club and Eastercraigs Youth Club.

This brought recognition from Celtic of specially-inscribed watches presented to the winning team by chairman Desmond White.

They also won the Scottish Amateur Cup for the second successive year, and in the three years they have entered for it they have been finalists each time.

The soccer philosophy which is applied to the senior team has percolated down to the Boys' Club. There is, for example, no religious discrimination in the choice of players . . . the only criterion is that they can play football.

And they apply a strict code of conduct to onfield behaviour. They did not have one player sent off last season, a tremendous achievement considering they run six teams.

Scottish Amateur F.A. secretary Leslie Michie publicly praised them last year when he said there was not a better club for on-the-field discipline.

Jim Torbett reckons to get around 150 letters a week from boys who want to play for the Club. And they have to organise a heavy programme of trials, usually around August, to pick out the players they want.

They are also snowed under with requests for fixtures, many of them for charity. And like the senior club that also brings a willing and ready response.

Jim Torbett says simply: 'We do our best, we try to get involved'.

But although he has played such a large part in running the club—sometimes it takes up every night in a week—the task is too great for one man to do it single-handed.

And he praised the committee he works with when he told me: 'We have a voluntary committee who get on with the work. They do a magnificent job'.

Their 1974 target is an ambitious Easter tournament involving 12 British clubs, six from Scotland, four from England and one each from Wales and Ireland, which will be for Under-16 sides.

And alongside it they will also run an Under-15 tournament involving six Scottish sides and European sides, with invitations already sent to such major football names a Real Madrid, Ajax and Benfica.

The competitions will be run jointly by the Celtic Boys' Club

104    . . . The cheque that helped to make the tournament possible . . . and it's handed over by an official of Barrs, the soft drinks company, to Celtic manager Jock Stein.

and the Glasgow Area of Youth Clubs, with an organising committee of officials from both groups.

Jim Torbett enthused about it when he said: 'The public at the last one showed that they are interested. People have sometimes said there is no market for youth football, I think we proved them wrong.

'The fans who watched us were not bigots or hooligans. There was no lunatic fringe. It was people who were basically interested in good football, and they were games to which anyone could go to take the family.'

So the blueprint for another busy season has already been drawn up. No doubt it will produce more youngsters who may eventually one day pull the green and white jersey over their heads to play for Celtic's league team.

But it should not be overlooked that in an age when youth so often gets a violent image the organisers of the Celtic Boys' Club are doing something to help kids . . . to give them other interests.

They are not sitting back on the sidelines and sniping at youth, they are helping instead of only condemning.

That alone is worthwhile!

# The cup that did not cheer

THE SOCCER sound barrier seemed ready to crack as referee John Gordon brought the 1973 Scottish Cup Final—Scotland's first-ever Royal Final—to an end.

For the Rangers fans in the giant 122,714 crowd hailed their team's 3–2 victory with all the fervour of supporters who had been denied for so long one of the country's major domestic trophies.

A defeat in an 'Old Firm' match is usually marked by the barometer of success or failure on the terraces. The winning team are hailed by a massed mob of their fans, not one of whom has moved, while at the other end the defeated side's supporters have simply not stayed to see the end.

There were some Celtic fans who left Hampden before the finish, but the vast majority stayed behind to cheer their team even though they had been beaten.

It was a sugar coating on a bitter football pill for Celtic, as were the handshakes from the players on either side who had just gone through again the punishing, nerve-shredding atmosphere of the 'Old Firm' fixture.

There were sincere congratulations, too, from Celtic boss Jock Stein to his opposite number in the Rangers team, Jock Wallace.

And there was a nice little touch from Wallace himself. He made a special point of shaking hands with Celtic's Bobby Murdoch, for as he said later:

'After we had won the League Cup in 1970 I raced on to the field to congratulate Derek Johnstone who had scored the winning goal.

'According to my mother who had watched it on TV I ran past Bobby who had stuck out his hand to congratulate me. She gave me a right ticking-off, so this time I made sure I didn't miss him.'

Celtic's players also found time to applaud their own sup-

porters who stayed, just as they had acknowledged them the week previously on a happier occasion for the club when they had clinched their eighth successive championship.

But in the inevitable post-mortem the question must be asked . . . where had it gone all wrong for Celtic?

They could point to one bad break, a debatable offside decision against Jimmy Johnstone when he had the ball in the net with the score at 2–2.

But that can only be an excuse, not a reason for the defeat, and the real failure lay elsewhere.

Probably their biggest mistake was their failure to capitalise on the marvellous bonus of scoring the first goal.

Jock Stein had pointed out the week before the final that the first goal was vital in any game, but it was really something special in an 'Old Firm' game.

And he added: 'Any time we have scored the first goal we have gone on to win handsomely in recent finals against Rangers'.

Celtic did get that first goal in 24 minutes after both teams had battled for the prize of possession in the busy mid-field.

It was a glorious goal, made by Jimmy Johnstone and Dixie Deans and pushed on for Kenny Dalglish to score.

That should have inspired Celtic, given them a touch of con-

108    **Dixie Deans heads for goal, 'keeper Bobby Clark slips, but somehow the ball stays out of the net during the Cup-tie against Aberdeen.**

fidence . . . but instead they let Rangers take over to boss the game.

The Ibrox side scored an equaliser which should have been prevented when Derek Parlane headed a goal in 33 minutes.

And the Celtic defence buckled again at another vital time, only thirty seconds after the start of the second half, when Alfie Conn outstripped defenders to race away from them and score a second goal.

However six minutes later Celtic did have a grip on the Cup again. Rangers skipper John Greig saved a shot from Deans goal-keeper-style on the line, and the penalty kick immediately awarded by Mr. Gordon was calmly slotted into the net by George Connelly with all the assurance of a 'Player of the Year'.

The fatal blow for Celtic came in the sixtieth minute. Their team was reorganised when Jim Brogan was taken off injured, and Bobby Lennox come on as substitute.

But Brogan's absence was at a crucial time. For when a free-kick from Tommy McLean on the left side of Rangers attack was nodded on to the post by Derek Johnstone at the right side of Celtic's defence there was no one guarding the other post when another Rangers defender, sweeper Tom Forsyth, raced in to put the ball in the net, although he later admitted he thought

OFF . . . and a moment of horror for Jimmy Johnstone as referee Bobby Davidson dramatically points to the pavilion with the controversial decision during the game against Aberdeen.

he had lost the chance.

So the scoreline had swung from 1–0 for Celtic, to 1–1, 2–1 to Rangers, 2–2, and finally 3–2 for the Ibrox side.

And in that last half-hour Celtic never really managed to put the sort of pressure on Rangers which would have brought them one goal to salvage a draw, or even the two they needed for victory.

For the neutral the best aspect of the final had been the good behaviour of the fans in front of the Royal guest, Princess Alexandra.

The fears that some of the worst scenes which besmirch 'Old Firm' games would unwind in front of the Princess had fortunately proved groundless.

Both clubs had gone to great lengths to warn the fans about the image that Glasgow would present to the soccer world if there was crowd violence, and happily the message seemed to get home.

Princess Alexandra enjoyed the game so much that she told Celtic boss Jock Stein after the game it had a better atmosphere even than Wembley.

But the final was not the only drama-packed match on Celtic's Scottish Cup road . . . I suppose the accolade for that fixture must really go to the fifth round tie against Aberdeen at Parkhead.

Celtic had started off in the third and fourth round ties— which are the first to involve the First Division clubs—by banging in eight goals.

They beat East Fife 4–1 at Parkhead, with goals from Deans, 2, and Dalglish, 2, and they followed it up with an impressive 4–0 win against Motherwell at Fir Park—one of their very few away ties in recent seasons—and the goals were scored by Deans, 2, Dalglish and Lennox.

Then came that fifth round tie against Aberdeen. The referee appointed by the S.F.A. to the game was Bobby Davidson, who had been involved in controversy with Celtic earlier in the season.

The pot was kept boiling after only eleven seconds of the Parkhead tie, with the waving flag of a linesman disallowing a goal for Celtic by Jimmy Johnstone.

It was to prove an ominous pointer to the part linesmen were to play in the match, and it was to be the start of an afternoon as dramatic as Jimmy Johnstone has ever had in his career.

The spark that lit the explosion came in 60 minutes. As the ball was played down the centre of the pitch Johnstone, closely marked by Aberdeen left-back Jim Hermiston, started a run up

Heads who wins . . . as Rangers centre Derek Parlane and Celtic skipper Billy McNeill both go for a cross during the Cup Final.

the right touch-line.

I had a perfect view of the incident, for although I had been following play, a colleague next to me in the press-box drew my attention to the fact that Johnstone was being held back by the Aberdeen player.

As they finally broke clear Johnstone seemed to aim a kick at Hermiston, which was more petulant than vicious and in obvious retaliation for having his jersey held.

Play went on, and the incident had not been seen by Mr. Davidson. But as the enclosure side linesman persisted in waving his flag the referee finally went to consult him.

After a long delay, and much talking between the referee and ·the linesman he called over both players and first of all booked Hermiston.

Then dramatically he pointed to the pavilion for Johnstone. The little winger appealed to him, but the referee kept pointing and the player started to run towards the haven of the dressing-room, apparently almost unable to believe it was all happening to him.

There was a nasty moment as bottles and cans were flung at

114     Kenny Dalglish raises his arms in joy, but this time the ball was deflected past and away from danger for Rangers.

the officials by enraged fans, and no matter how much they felt it was an injustice it is behaviour which cannot be condoned, for by it they put their club in danger.

Two other Aberdeen players were also booked, Arthur Graham and Joe Smith, in a game that had been an exciting Cup tie, sadly marred by that Johnstone decision.

After the game had finished in a no-scoring draw Mr. Davidson had to be given the protection of a police escort away from the ground.

But for Johnstone the affair was to have a satisfactory conclusion for him, after nearly a month of anguish waiting to appear before the S.F.A. Referee Committee.

For they ended one of the most controversial incidents of the season by finding the player 'not guilty', and no suspension was imposed on him.

However in the interval between being sent off and appearing before the S.F.A. his form suffered sadly.

He played in the Pittodrie replay, but he was a shadow of a player in another keen match settled dramatically in the way only the Cup can provide . . . with a last-minute goal.

Certainly they appear in league games, but they rarely have the impact that a late goal in a Cup-tie brings, with its joy for the winners and sorrow for the losers.

The man who scored the vital goal which broke the deadlock just as the game appeared poised for injury time was once again Billy McNeill.

He rose superbly for a corner, and with one of those wonderful goals which have been jewels in his career, nodded it into the net.

There was extra time in the next round, a semi-final against Dundee which promised to sparkle but somehow it took an awful long time for the cork to be pulled.

There was a drab no-scoring draw in the first game, when the Tayside team seemed to think they were still playing a league fixture and the prize was one point instead of a place in the Cup Final.

The teams were still deadlocked at the end of ordinary time in the replay. Then suddenly Jimmy Johnstone, back in the side and free at last from the shadow of suspension, broke clear and scored two goals, and Kenny Dalglish got another one to give Celtic a clear-cut 3–0 victory.

The gates had been opened for yet another 'Old Firm' final!

# My New Hopes
## by Jock Stein

HOW MANY MORE championships can Celtic win in this fantastic streak which has given us eight in succession?

That's the question which has been asked every season since away back in 1966 when we were crowned champions for the first time in my first full year as manager.

I accept that it has got to stop sometime, but naturally I am not ready to give up the prize yet, and I simply take each season as it comes.

I am even optimistic enough to hope that it may not have ended yet. And I feel now that we are even stronger than last season when we won our eighth championship.

Part of the reason for my optimism centres round two of the new players we have bought, goalkeeper Alistair Hunter and mid-field man, Steve Murray.

We bought Alistair Hunter from Kilmarnock because we were a bit indecisive in defence. He helped to tighten us up at the back, and by a number of shut-outs he contributed a great deal to the winning of the league championship.

For at one time in the race with Rangers it appeared that goal differences would be the decisive factor, and these shut-outs meant that the advantage in such a situation was always in our favour.

He has certainly done well enough to justify his transfer. And his experience of the sort of challenge we face in the league championship—plus a Cup Final début in an 'Old Firm' game—should stand him in good stead for the future.

He's a long-term prospect, and with reasonable luck of freedom from injury he could be the Celtic goalkeeper for the next ten years.

The mid-field was a problem area for us last season, and Steve Murray is the man who will be given the chance to solve it.

The mid-field problem was emphasised when I had to play the

116    The strain game . . . the venue, Easter Road, Edinburgh. As (left to right) coach Neil Mochan, manager Jock Stein, trainer Bob Rooney and masseur Jim Steel sweat through the last league game of the season, and the ninety minutes brought victory against Hibs, and an eighth league championship.

latter part of the season with David Hay—who is a better back four player—in the middle of the park.

He was out of position, and it was not to his advantage. But he did a job for me, especially with at one stage Tommy Callaghan injured and at a time when I was not prepared to risk young players.

However, Davie will be better for the team at the back, and Murray's transfer will help the team all round.

I know that sometimes Celtic are accused of being too canny with the introduction of young players, and it's a charge to which I would gladly plead guilty.

I like to put a young fellow in the team and tell him he's playing for two or three weeks, not just an odd game.

I will not ruin a youngster's chances just to satisfy occasional demands for new faces in the team. I certainly did not think the time to bring in youngsters was last season during the neck-and-neck championship run-in with Rangers.

This is the price we pay for the demands of success. Supporters

117

118 The strain game . . . the venue, Trondheim, Norway. And the expressions are the same as the men on the trainer's bench worry during the European Cup game against Rosenburg. The men with the problems are (left to right) coaches Willie Fernie and Neil Mochan, assistant manager Sean Fallon and manager Jock Stein.

were desperate that we should win the championship, and the situation was so tight we had to persevere with established players and keep plugging away with them.

But I think we are stronger now, especially in the mid-field, than we have been for some time. And I am looking for first-team challenges in this department from Brian McLaughlin and Jacky McNamara.

There is room too up front for players like Vic Davidson, who has already shown up in an odd game—such as the one against Hearts at Tynecastle—and Paul Wilson to make a consistent push towards the league side.

And, of course, the contribution of the more experienced players is not over yet by a long way. In fact, it could be even better in some cases than it was last season.

I know every season I say that I am looking for something extra from Jimmy Johnstone. But the fact that he played in only 22 out of our 34 league games shows that he should be more involved.

I do not think we will see a lot of him as an orthodox winger in the coming season. He wants to be more involved, and he's not doing that if he's lying idle out on the wing.

So he may play inside a bit more, just as long as it's in keeping with the general team pattern, and to the advantage of the side as much as it would be for Jimmy.

I know fans sometimes wonder why we do not go back to the formation which had two wingers, for if Jimmy does move permanently from the wing it will be the final break in the link from the days when we played both him and John Hughes on the same side.

The reason is simply that the mid-field is the engine room from where victories are forged. If you are outnumbered or outfought there nothing can happen up front . . . there will be simply no supply to the strikers even if you played with five forwards in attack.

One major problem we faced last year was our success in getting to three Cup Finals . . . and then our failure to win any of them.

It was a headache losing them. No one likes to be the defeated side in a Cup Final, that's for sure. But we could take some consolation from the calibre of sides we won against on the way to these finals.

The first competition we lost out in was the Drybrough Cup Final. I don't put a lot of stress on that because I don't think teams are geared up for such an intense level of competition

120  The face of jubilation . . . as the Celtic manager hugs Jimmy Johnstone after the little right-winger had been cleared of an ordering-off charge by the S.F.A. Referee Committee.

before the season has even started.

But there were some very attractive fixtures. We had to go to extra time to beat Aberdeen in the semi-finals at Parkhead, and then Hibs beat us in another extra-time clash in a high-scoring final.

Really in many ways it was too good a start to the season. As well as our semi-final Rangers had been beaten by Hibs in a spectacular clash at Easter Road, and I think the game of football took a long time in Scotland to recover from the effects of the Drybrough Cup.

This may not have been the fault of the Drybrough Cup. It was certainly the fault of the competition that followed, for we had to get on with the mediocrity of the League Cup which really meant nothing until the later stages.

Then we defeated Dundee after a third game in the quarter-finals, and beat Aberdeen in a good match in the semi-final.

But Hibs again conquered us in the League Cup Final. It was a good match, but on the day we did not play well enough to win.

In the Scottish Cup we defeated First Division teams all the way through to the final, starting off with a home victory against East Fife and an away victory against Motherwell.

Then came a no-scoring draw against Aberdeen at Parkhead, in a game loaded with controversy when Jimmy Johnstone was sent off.

That was not the only factor that disturbed me. It was the most trouble we had from the fans in any one game during the season, and that was as big a worry as anything else.

Billy McNeill's headed goal took us through the replay and into a semi-final against Dundee which promised to be such an attractive fixture but did not turn out that way.

I thought the replay was much better even though it took us to the extra time period to clinch victory.

We looked forward to our meeting with Rangers in the final, as we had been going neck and neck with them in the league.

Celtic had won the championship the week before the final with a victory against Hibs at Easter Road, and we were quite convinced that if we played to the form we showed in Edinburgh we would win the double again.

It did not turn out that way, for we never really played well in the match. Our best spell was at the start, and we scored a good goal by Kenny Dalglish which should have settled us.

But we never got the advantage of the composure which that should have brought, and before half-time we lost a goal started

122    The face of defeat . . . as the Celtic boss congratulates Hibs centre-half Jim Black at the end of the Easter Road side's victory in the League Cup Final.

off by a set-piece from Rangers.

And we gave away another only seconds after the re-start, although later we got back on level terms thanks to a penalty by George Connelly.

Three minutes after that we scored what I thought was a perfectly good goal, and television later on confirmed my opinion, but a linesman's flag was quick to indicate offside and a good goal by Jimmy Johnstone was ruled out.

However, having said that, I must also add that we never played to our full potential at any time during the game, and after Rangers got a third goal we simply never got back into the game.

It was disturbing to lose three finals, but it was heartening to win the major trophy we had set our sights on, the league championships which is the premier trophy and always the hardest to win.

It felt just as good winning it for the eighth time as it did away back in 1966 when we clinched the first one at Fir Park.

I reckon this was the most difficult of all the championships,

124　The face of annoyance . . . as the Celtic boss confronts referee Bobby Davidson during the League Cup quarter-final against Dundee at Parkhead.

and I thought at one time it was slipping away from us.

That was just after the New Year when we began to toss away points too frequently for our own comfort.

This was caused by a combination of factors. We went into the second half of the league programme with what was relatively our biggest-ever lead, a massive seven-point advantage, and I believe that caused some complacency.

But another major problem was the flu epidemic which sprang up to hit the team at the New Year period.

We missed two matches, against Kilmarnock and Morton, and then we played Rangers—and I'm not making excuses for the defeat—but we could have done without such a hard fixture for the first come-back match.

Then we had a transfer request from Lou Macari, and there was also my illness around that time which may have given the team the idea that things were running against them.

But there are no complaints from me that it was so tight in the final run-in. I've always said that we needed more competition, so I can hardly object when we got it last season.

The face of anger . . . Jock Stein leaves the terraces at Annfield Park, Stirling, after he had lectured Celtic fans for their misbehaviour.

125

Our fans became interested once again in the league championship. It was no longer simply a procession towards the flag but a blood and thunder battle once again.

That was shown in the very good gates we had for our fixtures at the end of the season as we raced towards the winning post.

I know some people think the Celtic monopoly has been a bad thing for Scottish football. Naturally I cannot agree for I consider that we have kept a high standard in all these eight years . . . I will be the first to congratulate another side if we still maintain these standards but are beaten by an even better team.

One disappointment outside the domestic world was our second round defeat by the Hungarian side, Ujpest Dozsa, in the European Cup.

But at the time we were just not good enough for the fantastic extra demands Europe puts on a team. However I hope we can make up for that . . . the major part of the prize of winning the championship is that the gates to Europe swing open for us once again.

And with it the chance to equal the side of 1967 who won the European Cup, and go one better than the side of 1970 who reached the final. These are the standards we have set during these eight marvellous years . . . these are the ones we aim at every season.

We do not always hit them, but not even our harshest critics cannot say we have lowered our standards and not tried for them.